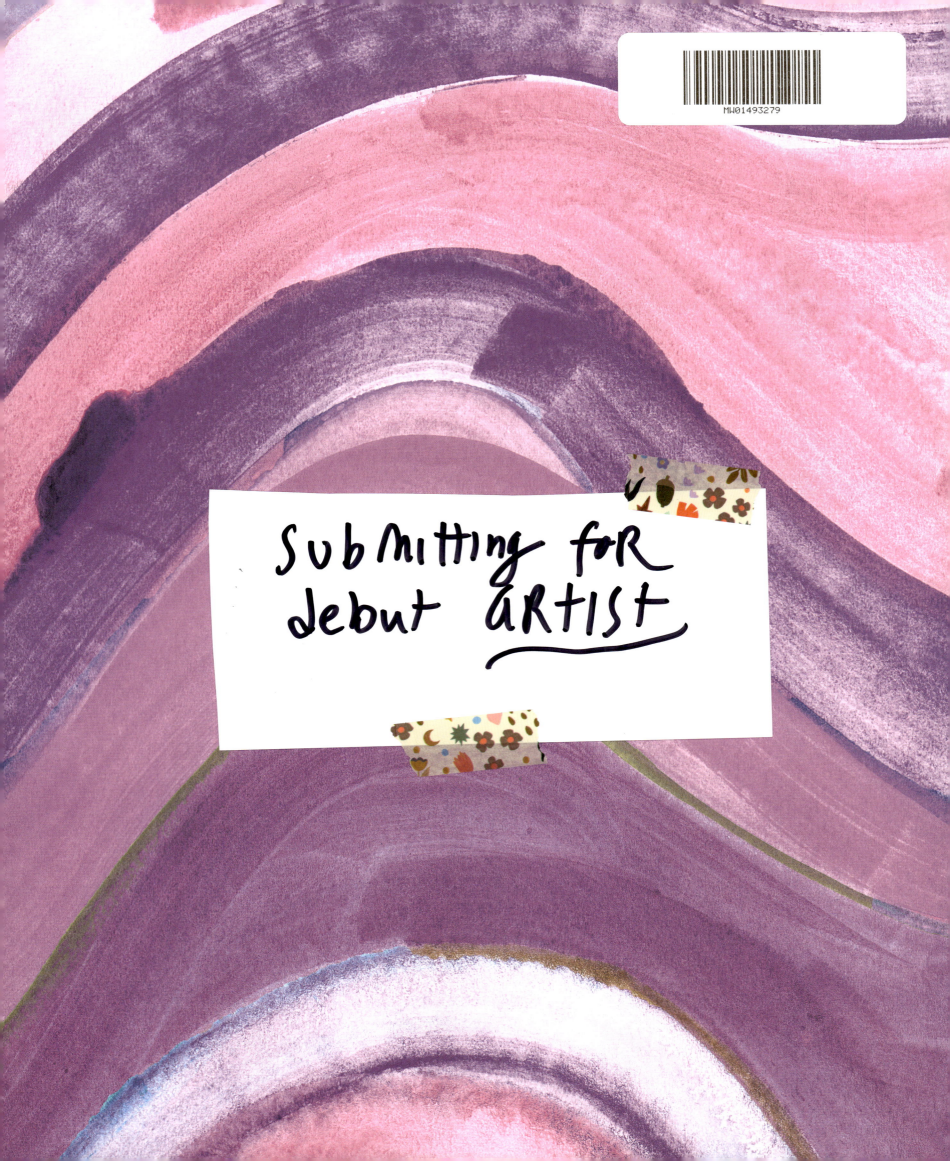

Submitting for
debut artist

*For the teachers, permission-givers,
and rule-benders who make spaces
where creativity can thrive. —MB*

*With love to Mom, Dad, Guy,
Jason, and Indie. —ST*

"I want to tell people to create.
Just start by creating your day.
Then create your life." —Prince

www.enchantedlion.com

First published in 2024 by Enchanted Lion Books,
248 Creamer Street, Studio 4, Brooklyn, NY 11231
Text copyright © 2024 by Matthew Burgess
Illustrations copyright © 2024 by Sirin Thada
ISBN: 978-1-59270-422-4
A CIP record is on file with the Library of Congress

Printed in China by RR Donnelley Asia Printing Solutions Ltd.
Distributed throughout the world by ABRAMS, New York

First Printing

FSC
www.fsc.org
MIX
Paper | Supporting
responsible forestry
FSC® C144853

WORDS BY *Matthew Burgess* PICTURES BY *Sirin Thada*

The Purple One

A STORY OF *Prince*

Enchanted Lion Books
NEW YORK

In a dark theater in downtown Minneapolis,
a boy and his mother take their seats.

He is the smallest person in the audience,
the youngest in the crowd by far,
the only kid in the room.

On a normal night he'd be in bed asleep,
but this is a special occasion because…

the man in the center of the stage is his father,
John Lewis Nelson!

The songs his father plays swirl and fill
the theater as dancers in flashy outfits
shimmy and shake to the music.

The people cheer, applaud, roar,
and for a few moments, the boy feels
as if he's floating in mid-air.

PRINCE ROGERS TRIO

8 PM   SOLD OUT

Prince Rogers Nelson was named after his dad's jazz band.
Something sparked when he saw his name in lights that night,
when he felt the music surge through the crowd like electricity.

Prince's mother, Mattie Della, was a jazz singer
with smiling eyes that sparkled and winked.
She gave him the nickname Skipper,
because he was so small and adorable.

But at school, Prince was teased for his size.

Few of his classmates realized
that this short, shy kid with a funny name
had a universe of music inside of him.

Music called out to Prince
and he wanted to learn how to make it.

He'd strike rocks together to create a beat
and pretend a box of newspapers was his drum,
thumping rhythms with his bare hands.

Once, when he disappeared in a department store downtown,
his mom knew exactly where to find him.

At home, Prince was mesmerized by his dad's piano.

It was off limits to kids, but sometimes,
when the coast was clear, Prince would climb up
and dance his fingers across the keys.

Then, one day, his dad moved out.

But the piano stayed behind…

A friend.

Prince taught himself how to play the *Batman* TV theme,
and at seven, he composed his first original song, "Funk Machine."

He imagined himself with superpowers,
and making music was the best of all.

When he was invited to a James Brown concert, a ten-year-old Prince jumped on stage and danced the Mashed Potato, grabbing the attention of the crowd and the great funk master himself!

As a teenager, Prince sometimes felt alone.

In the hallway at school, or in the quiet late at night,
he would pick up an instrument and play.

He wrote song after song, sometimes four in a day.

At fourteen he formed a band, Grand Central,
with his best friend, André Anderson.

Kids at school noticed Prince's talent
and in time, the teasing stopped.
He even earned a proud new nickname:
The Human Jukebox.

Prince started playing gigs
around town with his band.

Real-deal musicians on the scene
were impressed by this small kid
with enormous talent.

Chris Moon, the owner of a local studio, singled him out:
Can you add a tune to these lyrics I'm working on?

Surrounded by instruments, Prince couldn't resist.

He improvised a run
on the keyboard,

thumped a funky beat
on the drums,

laid down a groove
on the bass guitar,

and sang a cascade
of shimmering vocals.

After school and on weekends, Prince caught the bus
to Moonsound Studios and stayed for hours, even days at a time,
teaching himself how to make new recordings from scratch.

By the time he graduated from high school, Prince was a singer, songwriter, composer, and producer, and he had the demos of original songs to prove it.

All on his own, Prince traveled to New York City,
hoping to catch the attention of a major record label.

His plan failed. But this didn't stop him.

Prince returned home, found a manager, and kept at it, creating more songs and polishing his music.

Word spread, and soon people began buzzing
about this amazing young artist from Minneapolis.

Seizing the moment, Prince flew to Los Angeles to meet
executives from five major labels. One gave him a gold guitar
as a gift, and another promised houses in Beverly Hills.

But the most important thing to Prince
was the freedom to create his own music.

So he waited and negotiated before signing a record-breaking
three-album deal that guaranteed his creative control.

Prince was just nineteen years old.

Success didn't arrive overnight, and some people disliked Prince's flamboyant style and sound.

When the Rolling Stones invited Prince to open
their huge concert at the Los Angeles Coliseum,

the rowdy crowd booed
and threw bottles and food on stage.

But Prince was an artist and he wasn't giving up.

No matter what.

With his new band,
The Revolution,
Prince combined rock,
pop, funk, and blues
into a style entirely new.

He pierced the air with his electric guitar,
commanded the keys on the piano,
and with his voice…

Prince could croon,

shriek,

go deep,

and gently lift the roof

with his sky-high falsetto.

On stage, Prince was lightning and thunder bundled together.

He would strut,

do the splits and pop back up,

spin around,

kick the mic stand

and catch it

before it hit the ground.

He even leaped

from tall speakers

in high-heeled boots!

While writing his fifth album,
Prince noticed the color purple
popped up, again and again, in his lyrics.

Purple is regal.
　　　Purple is mysterious.
　　　　　Purple was perfect for Prince.

He started sporting a purple trench coat on stage,
and between shows, he wrote in a purple notebook.

His bandmates wondered what Prince was working on,
and then one day...

he announced that he would star in a movie inspired by his own life, and that he would write and perform all the songs on the soundtrack.

Some questioned this move. "Is he crazy?"

But Prince didn't listen to the doubts.

On the night of the premiere, when Prince was only twenty-six,
he stepped out of a purple limousine holding a purple flower
at the famous Mann's Chinese Theater in Hollywood.

The paparazzi's cameras pop-pop-popped
as celebrities reached to shake his hand.

Would the movie succeed? Would it flop?

Purple Rain became a box office blockbuster
and the soundtrack hit number one on the charts.

Prince was now an international superstar,
wowing crowds across the world!

But the road always led back to Minneapolis,
where he felt most at home.

So Prince built Paisley Park, a place of his own,
where he could live and make music
whenever inspiration struck.

Some songs he shared with other musicians.
Others he locked away in a room called "The Vault."

Oscar night!

Ping pong break

There were highs and lows in his forty-year career,
but within every challenge, Prince found a song.

In the words of Stevie Wonder,
Prince's childhood hero and later, friend,

"By following his own path,
Prince took music to a whole other place…"

Hall of Fame Induction

BATMAN Soundtrack!

When Prince was 49, he was invited to perform
at the Super Bowl for over a hundred thousand people.
The show would be broadcast to a hundred million more.

On the morning of the game, a heavy rain was falling.

The phone rang in Prince's hotel room.
The organizer of the event nervously asked,
"Will the weather affect your performance?"

With his
sly smile,
Prince replied:
"Can you make
it rain harder?"

During the first half of the game,
the rain showed no sign of letting up.

Fans feared the show might be canceled.

But at halftime, the stadium darkened.
Purple lights flashed through the raindrops
and with a blast of fireworks, Prince appeared
in the center of the giant stage.

His music surged through the crowd
while the people, ecstatic, danced
and sang along.

For a few unforgettable moments,
the stadium seemed to hover in mid-air.

Prince understood that a true superpower
is something you create out of love, hard work, and joy.

By following his own path, day after day,
the small boy with a universe of music inside of him
grew up to become…

The Purple One.

Author's Note

Hours after Prince died on April 21, 2016, a rainbow appeared in the sky over Paisley Park. As night fell, the Superdome in New Orleans glowed like a purple spaceship preparing for take-off, and in Australia, the Melbourne Arts Center was a giant purple finger pointing to the stars. NASA even shared a picture of a purple nebula "in honor of Prince, who passed away today." All over the world people gathered to share stories, sing his songs, and celebrate the life of Prince Rogers Nelson, the boy with a gigantic dream who grew up to become "The Purple One."

This act of becoming was no accident. It was a bold creative feat, fueled by Prince's tremendous energy and daring. In addition to developing the skills he would need to become a serious musician, the young Prince studied his musical heroes, wrote out the lyrics of his favorite songs, and made "vision lists" of the things he wanted to experience and accomplish.

Few are destined to become global superstars, and fame, though exciting, is not what really matters. For me, the story of Prince's development speaks to the creativity within all of us. "To use your gift in a creative fashion," Prince said, "that's the best thing you can do." Creativity comes in many different forms, and everyone has their gifts. Whether we create for one person we love, or one hundred million, the point is to use our imagination and follow the callings of our heart.

By devoting himself so completely to his art, Prince became a lightning rod for inspiration, and in his music, he's throwing off sparks. When you listen to Prince, you can't help but *move*. I hope you find your way to Prince's music, to experience his brilliance directly. There's only one Purple One!

Quotation Sources

"I want to tell people to create. Just start by creating your day. Then create your life." Prince. *The Beautiful Ones*. Edited by Dan Piepenbring. New York: Spiegel & Grau, 2019.

"By following his own path, Prince took music to a whole other place…" Stevie Wonder, in a tribute to Prince in *Rolling Stone*. May 3, 2016.

"Can you make it rain harder?" Prince, quoted in "Prince, In Memoriam." *The New York Times*. April 21, 2016.

"…to use your gift in a creative fashion. That's the best thing you can do." Prince, in an interview on *Larry King Live*. December 10, 1999.

Artist's Note

If I had a soundtrack to my life, Prince would undoubtedly be on it. Hits like "1999" and "Kiss" were always on the radio throughout my childhood and teens. Later, in college, my roommate and I had a special playlist of songs we'd blast when getting ready to go out. We'd be dancing around, trying on outfits, singing along to "Raspberry Beret" and other gems. It was a pre-party music ritual that would last well into my adulthood, and Prince was always at the top of the list.

It wasn't until 2004, however, that I began to appreciate Prince for more than just his musical talent. I was watching an episode of *Chappelle's Show*, when comedian Charlie Murphy recounted a hilarious story about Prince thoroughly beating him in a game of basketball, then serving pancakes to the losing team. Apparently, Prince was not only a musical genius, but had also been an excellent basketball player throughout his school years, and many have attested to his awesome sense of humor. Who knew!

In preparation for this book, I had so much fun diving into Prince biographies, interviews, and clips I hadn't seen before. And, of course, l had my favorite Prince songs on repeat while drawing and painting. The classic combination of colored pencil and aqueous media just felt right, allowing me to pair tight, careful renderings alongside the spontaneity of paint washes and blooms. Of course there had to be color and energy, but tucked away in the pages you will also find basketballs, pancakes, even bunny slippers, in honor of that other side to Prince that truly captured my heart.

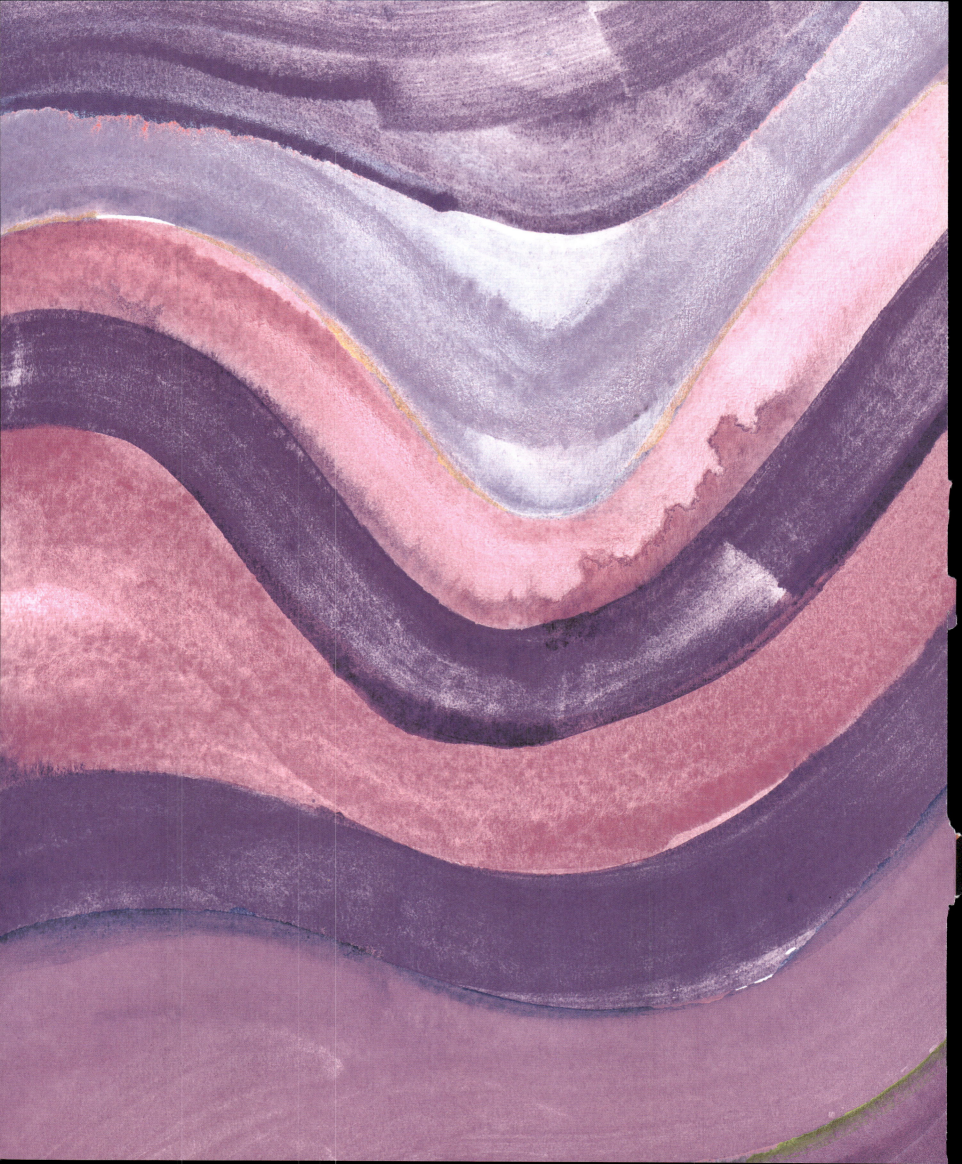